TOP-LEVEL STATEMENTS

WHAT ARE 'CLOSURES' IN C#

SARA JACKLINE

Top-Level Statements - C#: What Are 'Closures' In C#

Introduction

Microsoft's C # programming language continues to be featured in the latest SlashData Usage Report for the third quarter of 2020.

The report is "Developer Nation Originator Economic Status, 19th Edition" just released by research firm SlashData, which slowly implements C # 6 behind JavaScript, Python, Java, C / C, and PHP. ..

A year ago, C # was fourth, and in the second quarter of 2017 it was third.

While language usage has improved, "The way C # has lost three places in language network locations over the last three years is primarily explained by the listless improvements that occur in C / C and PHP. Will be. "SlashData.

Association meters are primarily used by requests for procedures with a series of audits performed as expected. C # was also not ranked in the 18th variant of audit when SlashData recently stated that it "seems to have lost control in improving the workspace, probably due to device advances throughout the stage." .. It depends on the progress of the web. The association says exactly the same in its new report.

In situations as large as a programming language organization, C # should be used by nearly 6 million designers, compared to 5.8 million in previous variants of the report.

The highlights of some reports related to the size of the programming language network are:

JavaScript is by far the most popular programming language, with 12.4 million architects using it.

Python surpassed Java near early 2020 with 9 million customers after adding

2.2 million new creators in the previous year alone.

Kotlin is one of the fastest growing language organizations, more than doubling since late 2017. "This year, Kotlin quickly gained popularity and attracted more new architects on the net in the 2020 core segment (400,000 vs. 300,000). Swift has become the default language for all Apple organizations to advance. So it was a Goal C decision. "In Apple's application environment, this reduction is further organized by a fundamental drop in Objective C status from the 10th to the 12th detection," the report said. ..

Here are some highlights of reports that are not related to programming languages:

Four in ten experts say that COVID-19 requires even greater diversity in working / service hours.

The gadget and collaboration phase is the most important prerequisite for engineers. By a significant margin, the majority of master engineers (more than 80%) are somehow affiliated with DevOps.

Constant Combination (CI) and Diligent Association (CD) are two of the most common DevOps practices. However, only one in four creators use both to fully robotize their work interactions.

Creators prefer to collaborate and discuss with their open source neighborhoods rather than adding open source projects.

Evaluation and support / documentation dominates the dynamic collaboration of professionals while embracing wool development. Still, quotes are the main excuse for making phone calls.

New advances such as AR and VR are not perfectly good OSS standards. Subtle changes in debt and paybacks indicate that DevOps has appeared in the trailer.

Miss / edge calculations provide a foothold among problematic planners, but in principle they are less responsible.

The 19th overall wave of developer economic audits was seen by more than 17,000 fashion designers in 159 countries between June and August 2020.

The report can be obtained in vain from the above associations after providing information about the registration.

First Programming Language

Compiling programs for your computer is an incredibly kind and rewarding drive. When someone sees you using a program you've put together to simplify your life, there are relatively few ideal assumptions that it really seems to make sense. Much more often, in the end, they wanted to have the option of actually accomplishing something with a computer or phone in their lives, and weren't ready to do so. There is a good chance that you can write a program that does the task yourself, hoping that you know the programming language. There are so many programming languages, but there are many similarities in their striking parts. This suggests that once you have learned enough of one language, everyone around you must learn another language sooner. Cut approach

One of the things that every new designer has to deal with is the time it takes to learn a programming language. In any case, once you become an expert, you need to set up multiple companies really quickly. You need to make sure that multiple companies are hosting an entire professional architectural conference that looks like eternity. So understand that knowing programming languages and some of them isn't enough to think of some of the most capricious companies I've ever seen. Don't see this new leisure activity as a way to save yourself a lot of money. It is out of your reach to provide your own version of most of the tasks you have to pay until you are notified later. Expansion.

The biggest concern that another computer programmer needs to know is that the book "Learn Programming in 24 Hours" is inherently wrong. The more accurate title is "Get programming in 10,000 hours". If you learn a language for 24 hours or 7 days, you will not be able to create the included Windows or other modern games. Nowadays, you can find a way to write a program. In fact, all you need to know another jargon is the main web crawler, but you're not an expert on this subject.

The most ideal approach to becoming an expert is comparable to learning to play the violin. The correct response is to exercise, exercise, and exercise a little more.

Choose your first language

Having considered the cutoff points and dealt with some of the weirdest suspicions, anyone who really wants a coding method will be pleased to understand that compiling a computer program is not really difficult. When. It's not when you learn. Offers you have to pay a huge amount of money. If you browse this article online, you'll have the resources to start with a particular language, so let's take a look at what the first language should be.

In general, the main language that first-year programming learns is Visual Basic or Python. The most important thing to understand is that these two languages are outside and there are several outside. The least complex qualification is the cost qualification. Python is completely free. At least for now, you can basically start running Python using the Substance Manager on your computer. If you're using Windows, you probably need to deploy Python first. Anyway, Visual Basic, which is usually summarized in VB, is free, not free. In addition, hobby VB learns by getting a license to collect interfaces (parts of the program displayed to the client) by sliding different parts in a similar way, rather than arranging some to organize. Can be difficult. Application work key. .. The variation they teach for VB beginners is usually Visual Basic 6, but anyway, it's a bit outdated. Therefore, these days, the variation learned is usually VB.NET, which is generally less basic for beginners.

VB.NET needs to be created in what is called an IDE (Integrated Development Environment). This is a special program commonly used to run a variety of businesses. These also exist in Python, but their use is completely optional. The free VB.NET IDE is called Visual Studio Express. The latest conversion at creation is Visual Studio Express 2010. Surprisingly, using the IDE free type limits the operations you can perform and makes it impossible to sell the tasks you perform financially. In a controlled manner, fully paid deviations from the IDE are unobtrusive and probably unsuitable for those skilled in the art. Fortunately, however, free structure is enough to teach VB. Finally, there aren't many business applications created in VB these days. In any case, the Visual Studio IDE can use multiple languages. The sharing feature you do with it also allows you to use the features of the IDE to promote multiple languages. Virtually any language can be a dust monitor, and some argue that this is the most versatile way of coding. This is very clear (and we encourage you to try to promote your materials research tools once they are improved), but it clearly encourages you to learn the first language in a real IDE.

People usually learn Python or VB first, which is commonly said in school, but I don't recommend both. Your first language should be important to you. That may have helped you become familiar with programming principles. If you want to recommend one of these to young people, it's VB.NET. This is because the most capricious part of writing a computer program is the graphics aspect, which is surprisingly simple as a natural result in VB.NET. interface. These two languages are commonly used as presentations because they are highly responsive to errors and allow you to review programming guidelines without worrying about more multifaceted topics.

For the fearless mind in you, I really suggest Java as your primary language, no matter how confusing it is in general, it's not the usual choice of primary language .. Java programs differ from most other programs in that they do not run on your computer. The client downloads Java and then enters code called a VM (Virtual Machine). This shows that the code is running in a staggering place where you can access Java compilation (a fake copy of your computer) and understand it on the right machine. The result shows that Java applications are "cross-stage" and typically run on Windows, Mac, Linux, and most other operating systems.

Java is a great language to learn because it is so comprehensive and very collaborative. What's more, it's incredibly nice and endlessly open to both professionals and business positions. Anyway, instead of VB and

Python, you shouldn't bother with bugs and expect to be very confident in everything. What's more, it's a programming language composed of articles, a surprisingly confusing topic that I'll try to summarize right away. Vernaculars like Python and VB are known as procedural terms, and Java is the mastermind of articles, while lines of code are presumed to be delayed one after another. Keeping in mind that object organization progression is a widely used term in the modern programming scene and is almost always inappropriate, anything that is considered an idea is a great idea. At the most basic level, the programs made up of articles are about objects. "Shipping" of "class" is one thing. A class is an airplane used to represent something like a cat. This class contains data such as the cat's name, age, and owner, as well as the "techniques" that are the basic exercises a cat can perform, just like meow. Class "Cat" events give you a specific cat. However, this is not a useful Java exercise, so if you have the courage to try a few things in Java, I'll elaborate on it myself. It is important that VB.NET and Python support the development of new object organization and that Java can be used procedurally. However, these are not commonly proposed basic habits and are not used often. If you don't understand the relationship, don't worry too much. This course is difficult to understand, but the basic information exercises in Java or other languages summarized in the article will help you understand all of that part.

Finally, Java is a good first language, and in some respects it is virtually identical to Javascript, a completely special kind of language. Javascript is a coordinating language (like Python), and learning Java means a fairly good understanding of Javascript. What makes the difference is that the coordination of languages and common programming languages is beyond the scope of this article anyway. Great theory scripts are commonly used for automated efforts, because customers use natural programs. Form. .. This is not entirely clear, as both types of languages are used for both attempts and most web applications use JavaScript.

When it comes to the real language you choose, it's generally up to you. Some choose common youthful words, while others are enthusiastic about trying Java. Some of you may now turn to one language or one of the more sophisticated languages like Scheme and Prolog. No matter what you choose, finding a way to program is almost the same.

IDE, yes or no?

Countless noisy people say the IDE is a useless idea, full of gimmicks and unimportant menus that take up space for cooking and learning. It's legal, but I have

Top-level Programs In C#

Adventure The new significant level statements at C # 9.0 to eliminate the standard code and make your companies more understandable, appropriate and useful. By forming programs in the programming language C #, it should never have an extraordinary standard code agreement, regardless of the fundamental control programs. Imagine thinking about some code to test whether a library or an API works properly. You can create a control community request to reach it anyway in any limited case to keep the standard C # semantics. You must create your code in the main procedure. Innemable level activities, another thought introduced at C # 9.0, give you code for SANS clear tasks the need to make a standard code. Innemable level obligations are a new extraordinary component that gives it to form a cleaner, more limited and less problematic code. You can include significant levels to investigate the soil that destroys considerations. This article discusses how you can work with unmistakable level companies in C # 9.0. To work with code models given in this article, you must have Visual Studio 2019 in your system. If you do not have a copy, you can download Visual Studio 2019 here. Note that C # 9.0 is open to the Visual Studio 2019 Structure 16.9 preview 1 or later, and in the SDK. Just 5.0. To make an inet core console application project in Visual Studio for a certain thing, we need a.

Just do core console application in Visual Studio. Tolerate Visual Studio 2019 is presented in its structure, follow the distributed means to make another application project. Only core console in Visual Studio. Send the Visual Studio IDE. Fit "make a new recad". In the "new care" window, select "Control Focus Program (Just Core)" From the summary of the designs. Break next. In the window "Orchestrate your new command", decide the name and region for the new search. Snap creates. Well, use this effort to work with significant level activities in the spaces due to this article. Significant level program model in C # 9.0 We must look at a previous period, then, at that time, at some point, the subsequent representation of how significant tasks can exclude the standard code. For important level advertisements at C # 9.0, it is the EDULA form of the Code for a Control Community Request: Use system; Name space idg_top_level_programs_demo { Class program { Head Void Static (String [] args) { Console.Writeline ("Hello World!"); } } } When working with C # 9.0, we can prevent the unmistakable level companies of RATTER and EDEA The increase with the code Show how it can abuse a significant level explanation to reject the previous code: [Learn how CIOS management reconsider it. Download CIOS New Think Tank today's report! Ary] Use system; Console.Writeline

("Hello World!"); But when the program runs, you will string "Howdy World!" See. It is displayed in the control area window. Use methodologies on unmistakable level tasks in C # 9.0 You can use strategies with unmistakable level companies. Next is a code model that addresses how to use significant levels of procedures. System.console.Writeline (Showmessage ("Joidip!"); System.console.READ (); static chain display (chain name) {return "greetings," name;} exactly when you perform the previous program, you need the performance "Hello there, Joidip!" Appear in the window of the holding company: Use classes in unnecessary level companies in C # 9.0 Can, according to class, structures and enumas companies in significant level companies. The increased waste code TRACE How you can classes in significant use levels. System.console.Writeline (new author (). Wisdom ("Joidip!"); System.console returns "Greetings," Name;}} Just when you manage the previous program, the show will appear on Figure 1 . How the unmistakable level activities are operated in C # 9.0 with everything that keeps in mind, how about work a precision significant level activities? What happens behind the scenes? Innemable level obligations are fundamentally a compiler function. If you do not make the standard code, the compiler will do it for you.

Suggest the march with the code of the piece we create before.

Use system;

Console.Writeline ("Hello World!");

The code below (made with the Sharplab Online Instrument) shows how the code provided by the compiler will look.

Use system;

Use system.Diagnostics;

Use system.reflection;

Use system.runtime.Compilerservices;

Use the system.Seguration;

Use the system.Security.permissions;

[Meeting: CompilationRelaxations (8)]

[Meeting: RuntimeCompatibility (WRAPNONEXCEPTIONHROWS = TRUE)]

[Assembly: Debugnabeatribute.debuggingModes.default | debuggationontribe.debugging modios.Disableoptiminians | Debuggies.

[Meeting: Security Permission (SecurityAction.RequestMinMimimimimim, Skipverification® = True)]

[Meeting: Meeting ("0.0.0.0")]

[MODULE: UNVERIFIC CODE]

[CompilerGenerate]

Static class within <program> $

{

Private static vacuum <Main> $ (chain [] args)

{

Console.Writeline ("Hello World!");

}

}

If you see the code provided by the compiler, you will see the quality [CompilerGenerate] on top of the static class made by the compiler. Innemable level obligations are a new unthinkable component in C # 9.0, so that the compiler makes the standard code behind the scenes. Significant level companies are unthinkable for clear activities that do not have a large number of records and conditions. Note that only one report can be used on your request important level statements; Regardless of the compiler casts up a screw. An obstacle to high-level level programs is that you, if you are new to C #, probably don't have the option to get what you're in the code behind the scenes. A better way for tender feet to learn C # will use the main method and avoid significant explanations until you observe how the capabilities of the main technique. However, people who overwhelmed the head will find an incredible level clear course. The best strategy to reach more in C #: The best strategy to use the configuration organization in C # guidelines to work with read-only groups in C # the best technique to work with the concealed boundaries in C # 9 The best technique To work with survey types in C # The best technique to use derivative and express directors in C # Singleton versus static classes in C # guidelines to subscribe data at the beginning of Windows in log in C # Guidelines for Use Arrapool and Memorypool in C # Guidelines for Use The Buffer Class in C # Guidelines for using Hashset in C # Guidelines for using the names appointed and optional in C # Guidelines for Benchmark C # Code

Using Benchmark DotNet Guidelines for Using Use of Recognizable interfaces and methodology limited in C # guidelines for the static test. Systems of the unit in C # Guidelines for refining the dissidents of God in C

Closures In C#

Stress endings in C #, including Lambda's strategies, specialists and explanations, so the code solid, capable, bright and less difficult to keep up. The terminations are often associated with utilitarian programming languages. The termination interaction The ability of its reference to the environment, which offers the ability to reach non-neighborhood factors. In C #, the terminations are maintained with Dark Systems, Lambda verbalisasies and agents. I analyzed strange techniques and [also in Infoworld: What is New in Microsoft. Just 6] This article explores how we can work with dark strategies, Lambda recordings and delegates in C #. To work with the code models given in this article, you must have Visual

Studio 2019 in its structure. If you do not have a copy, you can download Visual Studio 2019 here. Make a control application project in visual studio for something, we need a. Only core console application in Visual Studio. Tolerate Visual Studio 2019 is presented in its structure, follow the means described below to make another application project. Only core console. Send the Visual Studio IDE. Link "Make a new search". In the "New Search" window, select "Control Focus Program (Just Core) At the moment the designs are displayed. Break next. In the window" Plan your new effort ", demonstrate the name and region for the new search. Snap creates. Well, use this challenge to design the use of dark methods, lambdas and agents as terminations in the consequent parts of this article. A decision as a five-star in C # A decision is represented as a five-star feature that contains free figures related to the lexical environment. The programming language C # Respect the work of five stars as if it were a kind of first class data. It speaks that it can spread the capacity of a variable, it can mention whether it can give it in a similar way that works with a different kind of first class data. A provision is a specific type of limit that is intrinsically associated with the environment where it is referred. LTLiply can use the terminations the factors identified with the common environment, which is of these features that are outside the grade of the end. [Learn how CIO drive repeats it. Download CIOS New Think Tank today's report!] End Essential models in C # can put an end with a dark strategy as shown in the low-given code bite. Funt <String, String> Algafunc = Delegate (String TayVariable) {Returns "Hello World!"; }; On the other hand, you can make a determination using a Lambda function as shown in the code below. Func <string, string> algafunc = sainvaray => "Howdy world!"; Note that the two previous code remains a methodology that recognizes a string as a restriction and gives another string. Here is the way you can bring these two ends we just did: strstr = Alganfun ("This is a demo"); What about us, we look at another model? The piece of code given on the basis of a full number worth a factor without closing the name X.

```
int x = 10;

End of motion = delegate

{
Console.Writeline ("The value of the non-closed by factor X is: {0}", x);

};

end ();
```

Here's the way you can do exactly the same using a Lambda pronunciation:

```
int x = 10;

End of movement = () =>
{

Console.Writeline ("The value of the non-neighboring variable X is: {0}", x);
};

end ();
```

In both cases, the performance will definitely appear as shown in Figure 1 layer.

Terminations get factors, not features.

Since a final is linked to the environment in which it is articulated, it may refer to the expert components and things from within your body. Here's a model that follows:

```
int x = 10;

Movement A = Delegate
{Console.Writeline ($ "The value of x
is: {x}"); };
```

to ();

Just when the previous code is executed, the performance in the control window window will appear as shown in Figure 2.

The entrance to the Code Biet shows that the disturbing procedure undoubtedly does not undoubtedly the factors in the parent ethodology agency, not the properties. int x = 10; Action A = delegate {console.writeline ($ "The value of x is: {x}"); }; x = 100; to (); Exactly when you manage the previous code, the performance will appear as in Figure 3. Note that the disturbing limit 10, not 100 yield. How does C # terminations work? Just when the compiler C # a delegate that describes a final that moves beyond the current degree, the specialist and the linked area factors rise to a class of compiler. In addition, basically take a little compiler, witchcraft moves between the compiler's class events, ensuring that the agent is increasingly being argued, it is called a limit in this class. Once there is now, there are no references to the event of this class from now. The case is based on garbage by the GC, comparable, many cases accumulate. The following following is a summary of a class delivered by compiler, performed on the course of action of a piece of code terminated.

[CompilerGenerate] Private fixed class <> c__displayclass0_0 {public int x; Internal Void <m> b__0 () {console.Writeline (string.Format ("The value of x is: {0}", x)); } For a Lambda to stay "what can be called", the variables that have already executed the references of those who must persevere, even to the limit in which they were portrayed. To achieve this, draw C # in classes. Therefore, when a Lambda works a variable that is represented within a limit, the variable is removed and placed in another class made by the compiler. It's how a final capabilities!

SARA JACKLINE

www.ingramcontent.com/pod-product-compliance
Ingram Content Group UK Ltd.
Pitfield, Milton Keynes, MK11 3LW, UK
UKHW061705190726
13853UKWH00008B/2420